TAK

Do you need a business plan? Would you travel from your home to an unknown location without directions? You could but having a roadmap would make the journey easier.

The need for a business plan should be personal. If you want to map your goals to stay organized, then you need a plan. If you want to demonstrate your commitment and explain your methods to prospective stakeholders like a business partner, investor or lender, then you need a plan. Your business plan is a working document to help you visualize what you want to achieve. By using this guide, you can create a comprehensive business plan in less time than you think.

Take the Guided Approach

Are you one of those entrepreneurs who feel intimidated by a business plan and procrastinates writing it as a result? I am. I left my corporate job in 2004 and went to the Dominican Republic to spend five weeks learning Spanish and writing my business plan. I returned with about 5 pages of plan notes and a zero bank account balance. Without proper planning my entrepreneurial journey has been more difficult than it needed to be.

I wrote this book to enable entrepreneurs to easily convert their ideas into a coherent business plan. The Guided Business Plan™ is built around Action Items that are small tasks to help you create your content. It comes with electronic tools to help you format your plan and assist with financial forecasting. You may download these documents and connect with other entrepreneurs at guidedbusinessplan.com. The process is basic. **Write, research, edit, format, proof.**

And lastly, become a dream fulfilled.

Melanie Rae

"A goal without a plan is just a wish."

Guided Business Plan™

supporters of small businesses

Custom, onsite Microsoft Office® training to improve employee productivity.

officeleverage.com

Exquisite handcrafted jewelry for professionals wanting to leave a lasting impression.

kaiexpressions.com

Entrepreneur Self-Assessment

Take this self-assessment and reflect on whether or not you're ready to become an entrepreneur. Weigh the pros and cons for your situation. If you haven't sold anything yet, you may want to test your market before investing time in a business plan.

1. Do you have experience creating your product or offering your type of service?

2. Do people outside of your family and friends want to buy your product or service?

3. Do you have enough time to run this new business?

4. Are you organized?

5. If you have dependents, are they willing to sacrifice their lifestyle and time with you as you build your business? Are they willing to help out?

6. Do you have enough money to live on if you do not earn any money for the next 3 months? 6 months? 9 months? 12 months?

7. Do you have family and friends who will invest in your company or lend you money if you cannot obtain a bank loan or venture capital? Are they willing to invest now?

8. Do you have existing credit card debt or loans that would discourage a lender from giving you a new business loan?

9. Do you have a mentor who you can contact for advice?

10. Are you driven by passion or profit?

11. **Are you ready to become an entrepreneur?**

Guided Business Plan™

Written by Melanie Rae

Everyday Entrepreneurs Are Making a Difference.

The Easy, Simple, Guided Way.

BOOK SAMPLE

GUIDED BUSINESS PLAN
"A Goal Without a Plan Is Just a Wish."

PUBLISHED BY ENTRE TRAINING
~LOS ANGELES, CALIFORNIA~

THIS BOOK IS
DEDICATED
TO THE **BROKE**
BUT AMBITIOUS
AND THOSE WHO
SUPPORT THEM

Guided Business Plan™   © 2009 Melanie Rae

Written by Melanie Rae   Edited by Gloria Robinson

Cover and Layout Design: Melanie Rae   Photo Touch-up: C. Atoya
Photo Credit: Licensed with permission from Fotolia.com and Shutterstock.com

ISBN Number: 978-0-615-34001-2
Printed in the United States of America   10 9 8 7 3 2 6 5 4

Published by ENTRE Training, 1304 N. Highland Avenue, - 214, Hollywood, CA 90028
www.guidedbusinessplan.com   03311107

Guided Business Plan

We offer entrepreneur-education courses for
new and existing business owners.

guidedbusinessplan.com

Guided Business Plan™ is a 6-week online course catering to new
entrepreneurs who want affordable guidance throughout the
process of writing a business plan. We meet for 2 hours each week
for instruction, group support and work time to complete the
content.

bizexpressplan.com

BizExpress Plan™ is a 2.5 hour session to help entrepreneurs write a
condensed business plan to present to lenders or partners. It is for
those who want a concise action plan to organize their company.
We use the Guided Business Plan workbook to write the foundation
of the plan.

boomentrepreneur.com

Boom Entrepreneur is a niche Guided Business Plan course catering
to entrepreneurs over 45 years old. It is estimated that baby
boomers will represent the largest wave of start-ups who launch
consulting firms or small businesses.

layoffbouncebackplan.com

Layoff Bounce-Back Plan™ helps the unemployed become self-
employed. If you have been laid off recently and want to earn
income while you search for a job, we offer a free Empowerment
Guide and a 90 minute class to help participants land their first
customer.

Table of Contents
Action Items

BOOK SAMPLE

GUIDED BUSINESS PLAN
"A Goal Without a Plan Is Just a Wish."

Guided Business Plan™

Guided Business Plan™ Companion Templates

The following templates are used in conjunction with this book. Guided Business Plan purchasers must register via guidedbusinessplan.com to download the templates for free.

GBP Style Sheet   GBP Checklists

GBP Research Organizer   GBP Financials

*Templates are provided as is and are not guaranteed to meet the needs of your business. You may utilize them at your own discretion.

Directory of Online Resources: BizExpress Toolbar

The Guided Business Plan™ includes website recommendations at the back of this book. Links change and some websites become obsolete so we decided not to directly list the site address in the book. Instead we have posted them online in one easy to access format. We encourage you to download the BizExpress toolbar where you can find links to a variety of websites. Within this book, each BizExpress Toolbar link is denoted as:

BP : : Category | Link Name   *example:*   BP : : Biz Start-up | Legal Structure

You may download the toolbar from guidedbusinessplan.com. Once it is part of your browser, you can click on the **Category Name** and then the **Link Name** to access a great resource.

Special Thank You

To Janine Robinson, Gloria Robinson and Sofia Mahari
for *making it happen*.

What Is Your Wish?

In this chapter you will...

- Brainstorm your idea
- Answer the W^4H
- Revise your answers

Action Item 01.01
Five Basics

How long will this take?
90 minutes

Chapter Overview
Write the foundation of your business plan in less than 90 minutes. Instead of worrying about how to fill 30 pages with text and statistics that describe your vision, simply jot down your ideas. Answer the "what, why, who, where and how" (W^4H) of your business concept. It's all about brainstorming and then revising later.

Action Item Guidance

Write two to five word responses for each question on the following pages. Revise those responses into full sentences. These paragraphs will become the foundation of your Executive Summary.

Include quotes and statistical data to prove your statements. If you don't have the facts now, use assumptions. For example, as a placeholder you can write "X million people in Springfield, USA buy product XYZ". Once you complete your research, return to this chapter to revise your answers with accurate statements.

Make It Simple. Let's Get Started.

Reiteration Guidance: Start by brainstorming. Two to five words per answer-- that's it. In the **Tell Me More** section, revise your answers as complete sentences. Plan to spend about 2-4 minutes per question. Don't worry about grammar and sentence structure. You're just brainstorming.

What...

Business Concept **What**	Write 2 to 5 word answers
.01 What does your company offer?	
.02 What makes your company unique?	
.03 What makes your product or service unique?	
.04 What features make it different from what already exists?	
.05 What benefits will your customers get from your product or service?	

Tell Me More... Rewrite your answers above into complete sentences. This section will describe your **Business Concept**.

2-4 sentences

What...

Business Model	Write 2 to 5 word answers
.06 What product(s), product line(s) or service(s) are you selling?	
.07 To whom are you selling to?	

Tell Me More... Rewrite your answers above into complete sentences. This section will describe your **Business Model.**

1-3 sentences

Why...

Market Need	Write 2 to 5 word answers
.08 Why do you want to start this business?	
.09 Why do people currently buy products or services that are similar to yours?	
.010 Why will people be interested in buying your product or service?	

Tell Me More... Rewrite your answers above into complete sentences. This section will describe your **Market Need**.

3-5 sentences

Who...

Management	Write 2 to 5 word answers

.011 Who will manage the company?

.012 Why are they qualified?

.013 What positions will you need to fill now or in the near future?

.014 How many people will you need on your payroll?

Tell Me More... Rewrite your answers above into complete sentences. This section will describe your **Management**. *2-4 sentences*

BOOK SAMPLE

GUIDED BUSINESS PLAN

"A Goal Without a Plan is Just a Wish."

Who...

Competitive Position	Write 2 to 5 word answers
.015 Who is your direct competition? Which of your competitors sell exactly what you sell?	
.016 Who is your indirect competition? Who sells products or services that could be used as an alternative to your product or service? What types of companies?	

Tell Me More... Rewrite your answers above into complete sentences to identify your direct and indirect competition. This section will describe your **Competitive Position**.

2-4 sentences

Where...

Market	Write 2 to 5 word answers

.017 Where are your customers located?

.018 Where will customers be able to buy your product or service?

.019 Where will you promote your company?

.020 Who is going to buy your product or service? What do they look like? Describe your target market in a couple of sentences.

.021 In addition to your customers, who is going to benefit from your company's existence? The environment? Your community?

Tell Me More... Rewrite your answers above into complete sentences. This section will describe your **Market**. *3-6 sentences*

Where...

Operations	Write 2 to 5 word answers
.022 In which city is your company located and why is it a good location? Is it internet based or do you have a physical store?	
.023 Will you use outsourced contractors or will you perform most operations in-house with employees?	
.024 If applicable, where will you find key vendors to make your product or assist with the delivery of your service?	

Tell Me More... Rewrite your answers above into complete sentences. This section will describe your **Operations**. *2-4 sentences*

How...

Funding Needs	**Write 2 to 5 word answers**

.025 How much capital do you need to start your business and what will it be used for?

.026 How much money do you want from a bank?

.027 How much money do you want from an investor?

.028 How much money have you and/or others invested in your company?

Tell Me More... Rewrite your answers above into complete sentences. This section will describe your **Funding Needs**.

2-4 sentences

How Will You Operate?

In this chapter you will...

- Reflect on your processes
- Identify distribution channels
- Outline your operational cycles

Action Item 02.01
Plan Your Process

How long will this take?
30 minutes

Chapter Overview
If you're writing your plan because you need funding, what are you going to do the day after you receive it? This section will help you plan how your business will operate from the minute you get a sales lead to the follow-up after the transaction is complete.

**Action Item
Guidance**

Create an operational flow chart for each of your main business functions: sales, production, fulfillment and follow-up.

Does your sales process change depending on the type of product or service that you sell? Design a set of operational flow charts for each type of product type or customer group. Your sales process may be different if you sell to someone in your store versus selling to them via your website. You may also have a different process if you sell a commissioned product versus one that is already manufactured.

What's Your Daily Operational Flow?

Illustration Guidance: If you had a coffeehouse that you rented in the evenings, would you use the same steps to process a sale for a cup of coffee as you would for rental space? Probably not. If you're selling a cup of coffee, you may never see that person again and will not need personal information. If you're renting space, you would want the renter to complete and sign a rental agreement. In this chapter you will write down the steps you will complete when you sell, produce and fulfill your product as well as how you will follow-up with the customer.

You may have fewer (or more) responses than the space allocated. *Circle any example that applies.*

What product(s) or product line(s) or service(s) do you sell?

1.	2.	3.
4.	5.	6.
7.	8.	9.

What types of distribution channels do you have? Who will buy directly from you?

wholesaler   retailer   distributor   online   direct to consumer

1.	2.	3.
4.	5.	6.

How can a customer place an order?

phone   fax   online   at a store   home shows

1.	2.	3.
4.	5.	6.

What is your SALES cycle?

List the steps you will take when you are **processing a sales lead.** If someone calls you to place an order, do you enter it in the computer or fill out a form? If someone walks into your store and buys something, do you collect personal information? You may have a different data collection process if a customer buys online versus if they buy in-person.

Write out your sales process according to how the sale is placed. Include all the steps you would perform *until* you reach the PRODUCTION stage.

Steps in the Sales Cycle...

Phone

1. 4.

2. 5.

3. 6.

Online

1. 4.

2. 5.

3. 6.

In-Store

1. 4.

2. 5.

3. 6.

Other

1. 4.

2. 5.

3. 6.

What is your PRODUCTION cycle?

List the steps you must implement in order to **create a product** or **plan the service that you will deliver.** Include all the steps you would perform *until* you reach the FULFILLMENT stage.

Steps in the Production Cycle...

product or service 1 (name)

1.
2.
3.
4.
5.
6.
7.
8.

product or service 2 (name)

1.
2.
3.
4.
5.
6.
7.
8.

product or service 3 (name)

1.
2.
3.
4.
5.
6.
7.
8.

product or service 4 (name)

1.
2.
3.
4.
5.
6.
7.
8.

What is your FULFILLMENT cycle?

List the steps you must implement in order to **deliver the product or service**. Include all the steps you would perform until you reach the FOLLOW-UP stage.

Steps in the Fulfillment Cycle...

Phone

1.
2.
3.
4.

5.
6.
7.
8.

Online

1.
2.
3.
4.

5.
6.
7.
8.

In-Store

1.
2.
3.
4.

5.
6.
7.
8.

Other

1.
2.
3.
4.

5.
6.
7.
8.

What is your FOLLOW-UP cycle?

List the steps that you will implement **after a sales transaction has been completed.** Will you send thank you cards? Will you add the customer to a mailing list? Will you mail special discounts and coupons? How often? Include all the steps you would perform to stay connected to your customer.

Steps in the Follow-up Cycle...

Phone

1.
2.
3.
4.

5.
6.
7.
8.

Online

1.
2.
3.
4.

5.
6.
7.
8.

In-Store

1.
2.
3.
4.

5.
6.
7.
8.

Other

1.
2.
3.
4.

5.
6.
7.
8.

Action Item 02.02
Operational Summary

How long will this take?
20 minutes

Summarize your operations in one paragraph. You want to provide just enough information so the reader understands that you have planned your processes.

Operations	Write 2 to 5 word answers
.01 Where do you operate your business? List the city, state or country for all offices and factories.	
.02 Where are your suppliers located?	
.03 How will you assemble your products?	
.04 What type of packaging will you use?	
.05 How will you deliver your products to your distributors?	
.06 What type of customer service will you provide?	

Operations	Write 2 to 5 word answers

.07   What kind of follow-up
      will you implement?

Tell Me More... Describe your operations cycle. You may use your notes as a guideline or write your own paragraph. This section will describe your **Operation Process.** *5-10 sentences*

Action Item 03.01
Determine the Need

How long will this take?
75 minutes

Chapter Overview
Is now the perfect time to start your business? Is there a need for your product or service that is not being fulfilled by existing products or services? Use this section to convince a potential lender that there is a market for what you have to offer.

Who Wants Your Product or Service?

In this chapter you will...

- Explain the need
- Profile your industry
- Research your assumptions

Action Item Guidance

Write subjective answers about your industry. We are assuming that you have already done some qualitative research during your exploratory phase. You may have read articles about your industry, reviewed your competitors' websites, and observed your product or service in the marketplace. These are types of qualitative research. Respond to the questions on the following pages based on what you have learned about your industry.

You will have to perform research on your own to provide supporting evidence for your statements.

Use Our Links To Search Faster and Smarter!

Organizational Guidance: After you write your notes, spend a few hours to look up facts and statistics that support your subjective answers. If your reader asks how you came up with your financial projections or how you determined your market, you want to have the source information readily available. Invest time to do your due diligence and include your references in your plan.

Due Diligence

We have made it easier for you to organize your research on the internet. With millions of web pages, it's hard to sift through the clutter. In the back of this book, there is a *Due Diligence* section to help guide your research. "Due diligence" is just another way to say "do your homework/research" about a subject. We have also created the **GBP Research Organizer** to manage your data in an electronic format. You may download the template for free via www.guidedbusinessplan.com.

A Simple Process

- Respond to the questions within this Action Item based on what you already know about your industry.
- As you go along, write down items you know you have to look-up under the *Research Alert* in each section.
- Review your answers and highlight information that you are uncertain about or that needs supporting facts.
- If desired, make a list of what research you need to look-up. A Research checklist is included in this book. Check off the item once you find the answer.
- Use the website link recommendations in the *Due Diligence: Online Action Items* section to narrow your search.
- Download the **GBP Research Organizer** to manage your data collection.
- Return to this Action Item and revise your answers with your new found knowledge.

Industry Overview	Write 2 to 5 word answers

.01   What industry are you in?
        What is the NAICS code?

.02   What is your niche?
        Which sub-group are you
        targeting within your
        industry?

.03   How many people
        currently buy your type
        of product or service?

.04   Industry-wide, how much
        is spent on your product
        or service?

Tell Me More... Describe your industry and how your market fits within it. Rewrite your answers above into complete sentences. This section will describe your **Industry Overview.**

✪ **Research Alert:** What do you need to look-up online?

Market Drivers	Write 2 to 5 word answers

.05   What need does your type of product fulfill? Why are more people buying it now?

Tell Me More... Why are people buying your product or service? Rewrite your answers above into complete sentences. This section will describe your **Market Drivers.**

⭐ **Research Alert:** What do you need to look-up online?

Industry Trends	Write 2 to 5 word answers

.06   What are three trends
in your industry?

.07   What's going on in
your industry that will
change over the next
few years?

Tell Me More... What are some industry trends? Rewrite your
answers above into complete sentences. This section will describe
your **Industry Trends.**

✪ **Research Alert:** What do you need to look-up online?

Size and Growth	Write 2 to 5 word answers
.08 Industry wide, how many people buy this type of product or service? Collectively, how much do they spend?	
.09 What are other revenue opportunities in your industry such as emerging markets or new products to introduce?	
.010 Realistically, how big is your potential customer base?	

Tell Me More... What is the potential growth for your industry? Rewrite your answers above into complete sentences. This section will describe your **Size and Growth**.

✪ **Research Alert:** What do you need to look-up online?

Buying Patterns	Write 2 to 5 word answers

.011 How often do people purchase your type of product or service?

.012 Do your customers buy your product or service seasonally? Around the holidays? At certain times during the day?

Tell Me More... What are your potential customers' buying patterns? Rewrite your answers above into complete sentences. This section will describe your **Buying Patterns.**

✪ **Research Alert:** What do you need to look-up online?

Regulatory Issues	Write 2 to 5 word answers

.013 Are there regulations
or financial
requirements in the
industry that
discourage starting
this type of business?

Tell Me More... What regulatory issues affect your industry?
Rewrite your answers above into complete sentences. This section
will describe your **Regulatory Issues.**

✪ **Research Alert:** What do you need to look-up online?

Supplemental Section

Complete this section if it is relevant to your business.

Barriers to Entry	Write 2 to 5 word answers
.014 Is it hard to get into your market? If yes, why?	
.015 Is it controlled by a small number of companies? How many companies?	
.016 Do you have to pay high fees in order to legally start your business? Approximately, how much?	

Tell Me More... Are there any obstacles to get into your industry? Rewrite your answers above into complete sentences. This section will describe your **Barriers To Entry.**

⭐ **Research Alert:** What do you need to look-up online?

Maturity of Industry	Write 2 to 5 word answers

.017 How long has your
industry been around?

.018 Who are the biggest
players in your market?
Which companies
dominate your
marketplace?

Tell Me More... Is your industry new, emerging, expanding or mature? Rewrite your answers above into complete sentences. This section will describe your **Maturity of Industry**.

⭐ **Research Alert:** What do you need to look-up online?

Global Economic Factors	Write 2 to 5 word answers

.019 What is happening
      globally that could
      affect your market?
      Will it affect overall
      demand? Will it affect
      suppliers?

Tell Me More... What is happening around the world that could
affect your business? Rewrite your answers above into complete
sentences. This section will describe your **Global Economic Factors.**

⭐ **Research Alert:** What do you need to look-up online?

Action Item 03.02
Research

How long will this take?
2 to 4 hours

Set a work period of two to four hours to research answers that need supporting data. Use the Due Diligence section at the back of the book to simplify your online search. It includes website recommendations to help you find statistical information about your industry and marketplace.

Keep in mind that you will write about your competition later so this is a good time to make notes about your direct and indirect competition.

Notes

Who Are You Selling To?

In this chapter you will...

- Profile your customers
- Identify their attributes
- Describe your ideal customer

Action Item 04.01
Target Market Profile

How long will this take?
30 minutes

Chapter Overview
There is no proven method for effectively marketing your company. Observe your marketplace, evaluate your customers, and test various marketing ideas until you find what works best for your business. Before you start, you should understand who is making the buying decision.

**Action Item
Guidance**

Who is your ideal customer? Where do they live? What type of people do they hang out with? What do they spend their money on?

In this section you will create a profile of your IDEAL customer—the customer that you would spend money to market to. While there may be a range of people who will buy your product or service, there is a core group that you would specifically promote it to.

My Product or Service Is Best Suited For...

Illustration Guidance: A coffee house that sells beverages and rents its space probably has at least two different customer types. One group may be professionals who want a quick, hot, hand-roasted coffee to bring to the office. Another group may be entrepreneurs who want to hold workshops in the coffee house. Each group has distinct preferences and may need to be marketed to differently.

How many customer groups do you have? Divide your customer base into groups and name them below. On the following pages you will create a profile for each one to give you insight on how to market to them.

Identify and Describe Your Customer Groups...
You may have fewer (or more) groups than the space allocated.

Customer Group A	Customer Group B
Customer Group C	Customer Group D
Customer Group E	Customer Group F

Complete the tables on the following pages to describe attributes of your target customer base. Hints are included within the parentheses to guide your answers. Write N/A if the topic does not apply to your target market.

Customer Type (Group A) :

Write 2 to 8 word answers

Who live...
(urban area, within a radius, etc.)

Who buy ...
(type, indulgences, etc.)

Who are...
(job function, lifestyle, personality
trait, active, etc.)

Who spend more for...
(quality, personalization, service, etc.)

Whose affliction is...
(problem, medical condition, etc.)

Who are united by...
(support group, trade association,
social group, issue, etc.)

Tell Me More... What sentence best describes this group of target customers? Rewrite your answers above into one to two complete sentences. You will combine your Customer Type sentences to describe your **Target Market.** *1-2 sentences*

Customer Type (Group B) :	Write 2 to 8 word answers

Who live...
(urban area, within a radius, etc.)

Who buy ...
(product type, indulgences, etc.)

Who are...
(job function, lifestyle, personality trait,
active, etc.)

Who spend more for...
(quality, personalization, service, etc.)

Whose affliction is...
(problem, medical condition, etc.)

Who are united by...
(support group, trade association, social
group, issue, etc.)

Tell Me More... What sentence best describes this group of target customers? Rewrite your answers above into one to two complete sentences. You will combine your Customer Type sentences to describe your **Target Market.** *1-2 sentences*

Customer Type (Group C) :

Write 2 to 8 word answers

Who live...
(urban area, within a radius, etc.)

Who buy ...
(product type, indulgences, etc.)

Who are...
(job function, lifestyle, personality trait, active, etc.)

Who spend more for...
(quality, personalization, service, etc.)

Whose affliction is...
(problem, medical condition, etc.)

Who are united by...
(support group, trade association, social group, issue, etc.)

Tell Me More... What sentence best describes this group of target customers? Rewrite your answers above into one to two complete sentences. You will combine your Customer Type sentences to describe your **Target Market.** *1-2 sentences*

Action Item 04.02
Market
Demographics

How long will this take?
20 minutes

Describe the demographics of your target market. If you want to profile more than one customer group, draw a line to separate your answers.

Write N/A if the attribute is not relevant to the product or service you are marketing.

age range

What is the age range of your target market?

income or revenue

What is the income range for a household or the revenue size for a company?

lifestyle

What are the tastes of the consumer? High-end, moderate or budget-conscious? Are they family-oriented, do they keep to themselves or do they like to entertain?

affinity group

Does your ideal customer belong to a social group? These groups could be based on cultural, social or educational affiliations such as "soccer moms" or an institution's alumni.

geographic location

Where are your customers located? Are you selling to people within specific zip codes or on a regional, national or international level?

body attributes

This category applies to those who have a product or service that is based on a body attribute such as weight, height, body shape, etc.

number of people in household or number of employees

How many people reside in the house? Are there multiple generations? Include only if the size affects the purchase decision of your product.

gender

marital status

Single, separated, divorced, widowed or domestic partnership?

end consumer

Who is buying your product or service? Who makes the final decision? For example, babies consume baby food, however, the caregiver buying the food is your target consumer.

investment range

How much is the customer willing to spend on your product or service?

motivation

What is the underlying motivation for the consumer to buy your product or service?

ethnic group

Will more people of a particular ethnicity buy it because it reflects them?

number of children

Include the number of children that the consumer has if it is relevant to the purchase decision-making process.

circumstance
What personal situation is your customer dealing with? Are they part of a support group? Dealing with a medical condition?

buzz words
Which words did you find repeatedly in the course of your research that describe your target audience?

other
Add your own

other
Add your own

Action Item 05.01
Promotional Strategy

How Will You Promote It?

Chapter Overview
How are you going to let your potential customers know about your business? Where will you spend money to promote your product or service? What is your **return on investment (ROI) for each marketing strategy** that you implement? If you send 2,000 postcards do you expect an ROI of 100 new customers?

In this chapter you will...

- Choose your methods
- Write down your tactics
- Create a promotional action plan

Action Item Guidance

Think about where your customers typically frequent and how you will market your product or service. Place a ☑ next to each marketing strategy that you will employ in your campaign. You should identify strategies that you can afford now or that you will implement upon receipt of funding.

Write down the tactics that you will use for your marketing plan. Write an action item with a deadline like "send 100 flyers to target group by May 3rd". These tactics will become part of your promotional strategy. Include an cost and a potential (ROI).

Budget Your Strategies.

Write down the tactics you will use for each selected marketing method within the ADVERTISING category. Estimate the ROI for each tactic.

ADVERTISING	☑	Example: "Place a full page ad in the local newspaper for four weeks after launch."	Est. Fee/ ROI
Billboards	☐		
Coupons/ Flyers	☐		
Newspapers	☐		
Non-Traditional	☐		
Point of Sale Display	☐		
Postcards/ Banners	☐		
Posters	☐		
Print Periodicals	☐		
Radio	☐		
Sandwich Boards / Sign Spinners	☐		
TV	☐		

Write down the tactics that you will use for each selected marketing method within the ONLINE/INTERNET category. Estimate the ROI.

ONLINE/ INTERNET	☑	*Example: "Increase monthly newsletter subscriber base to 10k by April 30."*	Est. Fee/ ROI
Affiliate Marketing	☐		
Blog	☐		
Book-marking	☐		
Classifieds	☐		
Eblasts	☐		
Online Advertising	☐		
Pay Per...	☐		
Promo Codes	☐		
Search Engine Optimization (SEO)	☐		
Social Media	☐		
Social Networks	☐		

Write down the tactics you will use for each selected marketing method within the RELATIONAL category. Estimate the ROI for each tactic.

RELATIONAL	☑	Example: "Write 5 articles and publish in 2-4 trade publications by August."	Est. Fee/ ROI
Collaborations	❑		
Endorsements	❑		
Expert Exposure	❑		
Networking Events	❑		
Tradeshows	❑		
Word of Mouth	❑		
	❑		
	❑		
	❑		
	❑		
	❑		
	❑		

Write down the tactics you will use for each selected marketing method within the OTHER category. Estimate the ROI for each tactic.

OTHER	☑	Example: *"Include product in gift bag at four major tradeshows during Q2 & Q3."*	Est. Fee/ ROI
Company Collateral (business cards, brochures, etc.)	❏		
Press Releases	❏		
Product Giveaways	❏		
Product Placement	❏		
Sponsorship	❏		
Sweepstakes	❏		
	❏		
	❏		
	❏		
	❏		
	❏		

Action Item 06.01
Price Your Product

What Is It Worth?

In this chapter you will...

- Determine your product pricing
- Calculate the costs
- Estimate your sales

How long will this take?
20 minutes

Chapter Overview
Making money is the motivation that drives most businesses. We typically measure our success based on sales and expense savings. It is imperative that you invest time to develop a realistic financial portrait. Determine the price of your product or service.

Action Item Guidance

In the table below, write the name for each product, product category or service so it corresponds with a letter: A, B, C or D. Afterwards, review the Guiding Questions and complete the tables on the next few pages to determine the price and cost of your products or services. If necessary, revise your estimates. *Price Your Service* begins on page 51.

#	Product, Product Line or Service Name	Price	Cost
A		$	$
B		$	$
C		$	$
D		$	$

Determine the Price of Your Product or Service!

Guiding Questions

Material Costs

.01 What are the key materials that go into your product?

.02 What is the average price for each of the materials? Add them up and then enter the sum in the average material price field.

.03 How much do you spend on packaging for each unit? Do you provide branded boxes or bags? How much do they cost?

Labor Costs

.04 How do you define a unit of your product? Is it a single item like a bracelet or is it a combo product like a mug with a lid?

.05 How many units can you produce in one hour?

.06 How many minutes does it take to make a unit?

.07 How much would you pay someone per hour to make your product? Would you pay yourself the same as a hired contractor to do the same work? Enter the highest hourly pay rate.

Profit Per Unit

.08 How much money do you want to make per unit above the cost to produce it? What is the minimum amount that you are willing to accept?

Direct Overhead Costs

.09 Do you have to pay direct costs such as room or booth rental?

Distribution Costs

.010 Who do you have to pay in order to get your product in the hands of the consumer? Do you have to pay a commission to a sales representative? Do you have to pay freight charges to ship products to your distribution center? Do you have to account for freight and other duties? Enter an estimated average rate.

Write name of product or product line	A ✪		B ✪	
	material	average cost	material	average cost
Key materials for each product		$		$
		$		$
		$		$
		$		$

	A ✪		B ✪	
Material Cost Average price for all materials (per unit)	$	✪	$	✪
Packaging Cost (per unit)	$	✪	$	✪
Product unit definition				
# of units made per hour		/hour		/hour
Time to produce a unit		min.		min.
Hourly rate	$		$	
Labor Cost (hourly rate ÷ units per hour)	$	✪	$	✪
Production Cost (per unit) (labor + material +packaging)	$	✪	$	✪
Direct Overhead Costs (per unit)	$	✪	$	✪
Desired Profit (per unit) (minimum $ amount)	$	✪	$	✪
Distribution Cost (per unit) (minimum $ amount)	$	✪	$	✪
Unit Cost (production + desired profit + direct overhead + distribution)	$	✪	$	✪
DESIRED RETAIL PRICE	$	✪	$	✪

Write name of product or product line	C✪		D✪	
	material	average cost	material	average cost
Key materials for each product		$		$
		$		$
		$		$
		$		$

	C✪		D✪	
Material Cost Average price for all materials (per unit)	$	✪	$	✪
Packaging Cost (per unit)	$	✪	$	✪
Product unit definition				
# of units made per hour		/hour		/hour
Time to produce a unit		min.		min.
Hourly rate	$		$	
Labor Cost (hourly rate ÷ units per hour)	$	✪	$	✪
Production Cost (per unit) (labor + material +packaging)	$	✪	$	✪
Direct Overhead Costs (per unit)	$	✪	$	✪
Desired Profit (per unit) (minimum $ amount)	$	✪	$	✪
Distribution Cost (per unit) (minimum $ amount)	$	✪	$	✪
Unit Cost (production + desired profit + direct overhead + distribution)	$	✪	$	✪
DESIRED RETAIL PRICE	$	✪	$	✪

Price Your Service
Guiding Questions

Labor Costs

.01 How do you define a unit of your service? Do you charge by the hour? Per person served? Per project? What is your billing unit?

.02 How much would you pay someone per hour to provide the service? Would you pay yourself the same as a hired contractor to do the same work? Enter the highest hourly pay rate under Hourly Wage.

Material Costs

.03 Do you provide tangible products to compliment your service such as food and drink? Do you provide handouts, books or other reference materials that are not billed separately? Enter these costs under Tangible Products.

Direct Overhead Costs

.04 Do you have to pay direct costs such as room or booth rental while you deliver your service? This is separate from monthly rental charges. Do you have any direct costs that have not been accounted for?

Write name of service:

Billing Unit	per Person	per Hour	per Project
Hourly Wage	$	$	$
Tangible Products	$	$	$
Overhead Costs	$	$	$
Desired Profit Per Unit	$	$	$
UNIT COST	$	$	$

First Year Sales

Estimate the number of units that you will sell each month during the first year. Use the table below to write the estimated number of units that you will sell for each product or service line. Ignore the fact that some may be given away or sold at discount/wholesale pricing.

Enter your sales estimates into the **GBP Financials** spreadsheet to calculate your annual sales (available at guidedbusinessplan.com).

What is your start date to record sales? _____

Number of Units Per Month– 1st half

Mo.	1	2	3	4	5	6
A						
B						
C						
D						

Number of Units Per Month– 2nd half

Mo.	7	8	9	10	11	12
A						
B						
C						
D						

Other Considerations

The financial spreadsheet that accompanies this book is geared toward entrepreneurs with relatively simple business models. If you are an importer, exporter, manfuacturer, inventor, licensed professional or have a complex business model, you should understand all of the financial considerations that apply to your company. **We highly recommend that you consult with an accountant or other financial professional.**

The following are some, but not all, considerations you may have to include in your financial projections:

- Credit card transaction fees
- Duties
- Importing
- Inventory
- Quantity of measure – repackaging items bought in bulk
- Replacement costs – the cost to replace a faulty product
- RFIDs – ID tags for your product(s)
- Serial numbers for your product(s)
- Shipping
- Storage fees

BOOK SAMPLE

GUIDED BUSINESS PLAN
"A Goal Without a Plan Is Just a Wish."

The following are supporting documents that a lender *may* require from you. Refer to **Checklist K: Application Requirements** at the back of the book.

- Credit report
- Exisiting banking relationship with their institution
- List of capital assets and proof of collateral
- Resumes from key management
- Application (from their institution)
- Tax returns (up to the past 5 years)

Action Item 07.01
Marketing Strategy

How long will this take?
60 minutes

Chapter Overview
The purpose of the next Action Item is to help you create a marketing strategy to promote your company. You may want to include just a condensed version of your marketing strategies within your business plan and then put details in a separate marketing plan.

How Will You Market It?

In this chapter you will...

- Plan your strategy
- Determine your objectives
- Define your 4Ps

Action Item Guidance

It's time to outline your marketing strategy. These are the key components of your marketing plan.

PRODUCT:
Identify your unique selling proposition.

PRICE:
Write down your pricing structure.

PLACE:
Draft your options for delivering your product or service to the end consumer.

PROMOTION:
Devise a creative promotions plan. (see #05.01)

Create a Marketing Plan!

Product Strategy	**Write 2 to 5 word answers**
.01 What features does your product or service have that are attractive to your potential customers?	
.02 Why will they want to buy from you versus your competitor?	
.03 If you have unique packaging, how will it affect your product's position in the marketplace?	

Tell Me More... Why is your product or service unique and different from what already exists? Rewrite your answers above into complete sentences. This section will describe your **Product Strategy.** *2-4 sentences*

Pricing Strategy

Write 2 to 5 word answers

.04 What are your product
or service pricing tiers
or price ranges?

.05 Do you have volume
discounts?

.06 What profit do you
want to make per unit?

Tell Me More... What is the price range for your products or services? Rewrite your answers above into complete sentences. This section will describe your **Pricing Strategy.** *2-4 sentences*

Distribution Strategy	Write 2 to 5 word answers
.07 How will your product or service be delivered to your distributors, retailers or end consumers?	
.08 When is your product or service available for purchase? During certain times of the day or year? Only at specific events?	
.09 Where will customers be able to buy it?	

Tell Me More... Where will your customer be able to purchase your product or service? Rewrite your answers above into complete sentences. This section will describe your **Distribution Strategy**. *2-4 sentences*

Sales Strategy	Write 2 to 5 word answers
.010 Who does your customer buy from? A distributer, a retailer, your store or directly from your staff?	
.011 Will you use sales representatives? Is your sales force paid by commission, fixed salary or both?	
.012 Can people buy your products and services directly from your website?	

Tell Me More... How will you sell your products or services to your customers? Rewrite your answers above into complete sentences. This section will describe your **Sales Strategy**. *2-4 sentences*

Objectives	Write 2 to 5 word answers
.013 What do you want your marketing plan to communicate to your potential customers?	
.014 What do you want your customer to remember about your business?	
.015 What do you want your customer to do after they buy and use your product or service?	
.016 How do you want your customer to describe their experience with your company to someone else?	

Tell Me More... What is the objective of your marketing plan? Rewrite your answers above into complete sentences. This section will describe your marketing plan's **Objectives.** *2-4 sentences*

Action Item 08.01
Determine Your Costs

How long will this take?
20 minutes

Chapter Overview
How much money do you need to run your business? What are your start-up costs? How much will you pay for expenses each month?

How Much Will It Cost?

In this chapter you will...

- Estimate your expenses
- Research your costs
- Identify funding needs

Action Item Guidance

Review the Guiding Questions and verbally answer them. Use the expenses table on the next pages as a guide to list your responses. You may want to add or ignore expenses from this list. Use the **GBP Financials** spreadsheet to enter your sales and expenses and to project your cash flow. It is available at www.guidedbusinessplan.com.

Who Do You Have to Pay?

Guiding Questions

.01 Will you lease an office or set-up a home office?

.02 Will you rent meeting space?

.03 Do you need letterhead? Business cards? Office supplies? Other stationery?

.04 Do you need to acquire furniture? Do you have enough desk space? Workroom tables?

.05 Do you expect to spend a large amount on postage?

.06 What are your utility costs composed of? Cell phones? Landlines? Electricity? Cable?

.07 Do you need to include software purchases in your budget? Do you need to get additional licenses for desktop applications? Will you use an online subscription application such as salesforce.com®?

.08 What office equipment will you need such as computers, fax machines, and phones?

.09 Do you have to factor in sales commission as part of your expenses? If yes, leave this line blank and enter the rate on the GBP Financials spreadsheet.

.010 How much will you spend on your marketing budget? (Estimate your numbers for now and then compile accurate numbers when you create a marketing plan.)

.011 Do you plan to hire a consultant to grow your business? Do you need to pay professional retainers?

.012 Do you need to purchase equipment to manufacture your product? Do you need specialized equipment to deliver your service?

.013   Do you need to pay for legal services? Are you going to have a lawyer on retainer?

.014   What type of insurance do you need for your company? General liability? Workers compensation? Health insurance?

.015   Are you going to have a monthly allowance for car and mileage expenses? Other travel expenses?

.016   How much will you allocate for membership dues to trade associations and subscriptions to trade publications?

.017   Do you have any annual credit card fees?

.018   Do you plan to donate a portion of your proceeds to charity on a regular basis? Is there a minimum that you will donate?

.019   Do you need to invest in a website? Is it the cornerstone of your business or an informational tool?

.020   Do you have to pay for monthly hosting fees for your website?

.021   Do you have a merchant account? Is it a flat fee or do they charge per month or per transaction?

.022   How much do you want to save each month for reserves?

.023   Do you have tax payments for the previous year?

.024   Are you going to give yourself an owner's stipend or withdrawal? In other words, are you going to pay yourself each month?

.025   Do you have to repay any loans?

.026   Do you have interest payments?

.027   What are your quarterly tax payments for the current year?

.028   Do you have any other expenses or payments that are not accounted for?

Determine Your Costs

Enter your estimated costs in the table below or type them directly into the **GBP Financials** spreadsheet. If the expense only occurs when you're setting up your business, place it in the Start-up column. If it is ongoing, then place it in the Monthly column.

	Office Expenses	Start-up	Monthly
0.1	Office Lease/Home Office Rent	$	$
0.2	Meeting Space Rent	$	$
0.3	Stationery and Office Supplies	$	$
0.4	Furniture	$	$
0.5	Postage	$	$
0.6	Utilities	$	$
0.7	Software	$	$
0.8	Office Equipment	$	$
0.9	Sales Costs (commission %)	%	%
0.10	Marketing	$	$
0.11	Professional Fees	$	$
0.12	Equipment	$	$
0.13	Legal	$	$

	Office Expenses	Start-up	Monthly
0.14	Insurance	$	$
0.15	Travel	$	$
0.16	Dues & Subscriptions	$	$
0.17	Credit Card Fees	$	$
0.18	Charitable Contributions	$	$
0.19	Web Design & Maintenance	$	$
0.20	Website Hosting	$	$
0.21	Merchant Account	$	$
0.22	Reserves	$	$
0.23	Other Taxes	$	$
0.24	Owner's Withdrawal	$	$
0.25	Loan Repayment	$	$
0.26	Interest Payment	$	$
0.27	Current Year Tax Payments	$	$
0.28	Other Payments	$	$
0.29	Other Payments	$	$

Assumptions

Readers will want to understand any projections that are based on assumptions. For example, if you think your sales will increase dramatically during the holiday season, then you should add a note that your sales cycle is between August and January. Another example may be that you won't start paying yourself a salary until Year 2 which explains why costs are greater than the previous year. In your business plan, you should include a list of your assumptions under your financial data tables or charts.

You may use the space below to write any notes for your financial assumptions.

Action Item 08.02
Funding Sources

How long will this take?
20 minutes

Do you know how much money you need to get started and to sustain your operations for the first couple of years? Do you want to take out a loan or are you looking for an investor? An investor is going to want to realize a return that is more than what they would receive from a less risky investment. It's important to weigh the pros and cons of taking on debt or giving out equity in your business.

While it may seem like you answered this question before, keep in mind that most readers will not read your entire plan. They probably want to know the answer to "how much do they want?" Your funding request should be featured in a couple of sections within your plan.

Funding Needs	Write 2 to 5 word answers
.01 How much money has already been invested by you, your partner and/or third parties?	
.02 How much money are you seeking from investors?	
.03 How much money do you want to borrow?	
.04 What are you willing to give to investors? Company ownership? An attractive return on investment?	
.05 When will they start receiving dividends or principal payments?	

Tell Me More... What are your funding needs? What will your lender or investor receive? Rewrite the answers above into complete sentences. This section will describe your **Funding Needs** for inclusion in your Financials section. *2-4 sentences*

Exit Strategy	Write 2 to 5 word answers
.06 Do you plan to own and manage your company for a specific time period? If yes, what is your time frame?	
.07 What type of buyers would be interested in buying your company?	
.08 How much money do you want to sell your company for?	
.09 Do you want to bequeath your company to an heir?	
.010 Do you think you want to grow your company by acquiring others? If yes, what type of companies?	BOOK SAMPLE GUIDED BUSINESS PLAN "A Goal Without a Plan Is Just a Wish."

Tell Me More... What is your exit strategy? Rewrite your answers above into complete sentences. This section will describe your **Exit Strategy** for inclusion in your Executive Summary section.
2-4 sentences

Action Item 09.01
Competition

Who's Your Competition?

In this chapter you will...

- Identify direct competitors
- Summarize indirect competition
- Evaluate your SWOT

How long will this take?
50 minutes

Chapter Overview
There's a lot you can learn from your competitors to help you grow your company. Avoid their mistakes and improve upon their strategies. At the very least you should know who your closest competition is and monitor their activities so you can offer better customer satisfaction.

Action Item Guidance

Write subjective answers about your competition. Have you read articles about your industry? Reviewed your competitors' websites? Observed their products or services in the marketplace? Respond to the questions on the following pages based on what you have learned about the competition in your industry.

Plan to spend a few hours to look- up facts and statistics that support your subjective answers. Refer to the **Due Diligence** section to streamline your internet search.

How Do You Compare With Your Competitors?

Competitive Position	Write 2 to 5 word answers

.01   What is your
       competitive advantage
       over your
       competition?

Tell Me More... What does your company have that will make you stand out from your competition? Rewrite your answer above into complete sentences. This section will describe your **Competitive Position.** *2-4 sentences*

Direct Competition	Write 2 to 5 word answers

Who do you think your direct competitors are?

Write a brief description of each of your top four competitors and indicate your competitive advantage. *Hint: Copy their company description from their website and reference it in your footnotes.*

.02   Competitor Name (1)

Direct Competition

.03   Competitor Name (2)

.04   Competitor Name (3)

.05   Competitor Name (4)

Direct Competition	Write 2 to 5 word answers

Tell Me More... Who are your direct competitors? Rewrite your answers above into complete sentences. This section will describe your **Direct Competitors.** *4-10 sentences*

Indirect Competition	Write 2 to 5 word answers
.06 Who do you think your indirect competitors are? In other words, what could people buy as an alternative to your product or service?	
.07 What or who is your future competition?	
.08 How do you address future competition?	

Tell Me More... Who are your indirect competitors? What are their websites? How will you categorize them? This may be subjective. Rewrite your answers above into complete sentences. This section will describe your **Indirect Competitors.** *3-5 sentences*

Action Item 09.02
SWOT

How long will this take?
60 minutes

To support your elevator pitch, you should be able to answer any questions that your audience may raise. What are your company's **strengths**? What are your **weaknesses**? What are the **opportunities** in your marketplace? What are some **threats** facing your industry? Collectively, this is known as a **SWOT** analysis.

Strengths	Write 2 to 5 word answers
.01	In general, why do you have an edge over your competitors?
.02	What differentiates your management team?
.03	What processes, technology or vendors do you have in place that will make you different from your competitors?

Tell Me More... What are your company's strengths? Rewrite your answers above into a bulleted list. Include additional strengths if desired. This section will describe your **Strengths**. *3-6 bullets*

Weaknesses	Write 2 to 5 word answers

.04   Does your management team have any weaknesses that should be addressed?

.05   Do you have any obstacles that you need to overcome during your first year of operations?

Tell Me More... What are your company's weaknesses? Rewrite your answers above into a bulleted list. Include additional weaknesses if desired but provide a solution as well. This section will describe your **Weaknesses.** *3-6 bullets*

Opportunities	Write 2 to 5 word answers
.06 What changes are happening within your industry that makes this a good time to start your business?	
.07 What relationships have you formed that will create more opportunities for you?	

Tell Me More... What are some pending opportunities for your company? What are some opportunities for your industry? Rewrite your answers above into a bulleted list. Include additional opportunities if desired. This section will describe your **Opportunities.** *3-6 bullets*

Threats	**Write 2 to 5 word answers**

.08   What are three key issues facing your industry?

.09   Do environmental factors have an impact on your business or industry?

.010 What alternative products or services can your ideal customer buy instead of yours and how does this impact your business?

Tell Me More... What are some threats that face your business and market? Rewrite your answers above into a bulleted list. Include additional threats if desired. This section will describe your **Threats**. *3-6 bullets*

What Do You Want Next?

In this chapter you will...

- Summarize your vision
- Discuss other opportunities
- Reiterate your strengths

How long will this take?
45 minutes

Chapter Overview
The final stretch. It's time to summarize your plan and make a compelling argument for why stakeholders should become involved in your project.

**Action Item
Guidance**

Tell the reader about your strengths and accomplishments. Intrigue them with your expansion ideas and potential collaborations. Finally, reiterate what you are looking for and what you want the reader to do.

You may find that your funding requests are repeated in your plan. You want to make it easy for the reader to know how much you want, from whom, and what you will use it for. Your funding needs are stated in your Executive Summary, Finacials and Summary sections.

Create a Call to Action!

Summary	Write 10 words or fewer
.01 What is your business concept and why would a lender or investor be interested in what you have to offer?	
.02 What are the most important messages that you want the reader to remember about your business?	

Tell Me More... What do you want the reader to remember about your plan? Rewrite your answers above into complete sentences. This section will describe your **Summary.** *3-5 sentences*

Expansion Opportunities...	Write 2 to 5 word answers
.03 What are some consumer markets that you may try to penetrate in the future?	
.04 What are some ideas that you have to diversify your product line? Will you sell new products or the same one with different attributes?	
.05 Are there any marketing opportunities or economic shifts that could greatly increase your brand awareness?	

Tell Me More... What are some of your expansion opportunities? Rewrite your answers above into complete sentences. This section will describe your **Expansion Opportunities.** *2-4 sentences*

Keys to Success	Write 2 to 5 word answers
.06 What have you accomplished to date that is enticing to a potential stakeholder?	
.07 What makes your management team exceptional?	
.08 Is your product or service process hard to duplicate? If yes, why?	
.09 Do you have endorsements from industry influencers?	

Tell Me More... What have you accomplished to date that is enticing to a potential stakeholder? Rewrite your answers above into complete sentences. This section will describe your **Keys To Success.** *3-6 sentences*

Funds Sought | Write 2 to 5 word answers

.010 What is the company's development stage? Are you looking for seed money to start your business or working capital to expand your business?

.011 Who are you looking for funding from?

.012 How much money are you seeking?

.013 What will the money go towards? For example, are you buying inventory, equipment or funding payroll?

.014 How much revenue do you project to earn in year 1? In year 2?

Tell Me More... Write a summary of the funds that you are seeking. What is your timeline for repayment? Rewrite your answers above into complete sentences. This section will describe your **Funds Sought** for inclusion in your Summary section.
2-4 sentences

Contact Information	Write 2 to 5 word answers

.015 What is the contact information for the person managing your financial capital?

Tell Me More... Who should the reader contact for more information? Format the contact information accordingly. This section will describe your **Contact Information.**

Notes

Action Item 11.01
Company Background

What's Your Background?

In this chapter you will...

- List your company details
- Write a mission statement
- Revise your answers

How long will this take?
20 minutes

Chapter Overview
Create your company's identity. Define your guiding principles from the start to help develop your brand.

BOOK SAMPLE

GUIDED BUSINESS PLAN
"A Goal Without a Plan Is Just a Wish."

Action Item Guidance

Information about your Company Background will be placed toward the beginning of your business plan. This is like a fact sheet that describes your company at a glance. Your responses should be short and concise. A few samples are included to demonstrate how short your answers should be.

Tell Us About Your Company!

Company Background	Heading Title	Write 2 to10 word answers

Combine your answers from #1 to #2 to describe your Company Description and Legal Name.

Example: Company Description
[Legal Name of Company] is a [adjective] firm that services the [target market description] market with [product name or type].

.01	What services or products does your company provide and who do you sell them to?	Company Description	
.02	What is your company's legal name?	Legal Name	

Company History

If you have an existing company, briefly describe its history including key contracts and milestones.

Combine your answers from #3 to #7 to describe your Company Ownership and Legal Structure.

Example: Company Ownership & Legal Structure
[Name] is the founder and CEO of the company and will oversee all aspects of the development of the company. She retains 100% ownership. The company was founded in [year] and is a [legal structure] governed by the laws of the state of Washington.

.03	What year was your company founded?	Company Ownership and Legal Structure	
.04	Who are the founders of the company? What are their titles?	Company Ownership and Legal Structure	

Company Background		Heading Title	Write 2 to10 word answers
.05	Who owns the company? What is the ownership percentage?	Company Ownership and Legal Structure	
.06	What is the legal structure of your company?	Company Ownership and Legal Structure	
.07	In which state did you register your business?	Company Ownership and Legal Structure	

Combine your answers from #8 to #9 to describe your Names of Top Management.

Example: Names of Top Management
[Name withheld] is the Chief Executive Officer and [Functional Job Title]. [Company] currently has [number] full-time employees. [Name], [Job Title], and [Name], [Job Title].

.08	How many employees do you currently have?	Names of Top Management	
.09	Who are key members of your management team? What are their titles?	Names of Top Management	

Combine your answers from #10 to #11 to describe your Location and Geographical Information.

Example: Location and Geographical Information
[Company] is headquartered in [city, state]. We have satellite offices in [city, state] and work with manufacturers in [city, state].

OR

Company Background	Heading Title	Write 2 to10 word answers

Each of the key personnel operates from a home office in the [city, state] area. The company has a centralized warehouse in [city] for [purpose]. We distribute our products internationally through retail, wholesale and direct to consumer outlets.

.010 Where is your company headquartered?	Location and Geographical Information	
.011 Does your company have any other offices, factories or buildings? Where?	Location and Geographical Information	
.012 What licenses and permits are required? Which ones do you have? Do you have any certifications?	Trademark, Copyright, Domain Name and Other Information	
.013 What trademarks, copyrights or patents does your company hold?	Trademark, Copyright, Domain Name and Other Information	
.014 What domain names have been registered?	Trademark, Copyright, Domain Name and Other Information	
.015 What is your company's logo(s)?	Include your logo in your plan	

Company Background	Heading Title	
.016 What products or services does your company offer? This section should include product descriptions and sample pictures. What are the features and benefits of your product? Use the **GBP Style Sheet** to type your description. You may include product photos as well.	Products/ Services	

Action Item 11.02
Mission Statement

How long will this take?
15 minutes

Before completing your plan, you should write a mission statement that conveys your company's guiding principles. It is a one to three sentence mantra that unites your employees to work toward a common goal and reiterates the true benefits of your services to your customers.

Supplemental Section

Complete this section if it is relevant to your business.

Concisely answer the following questions with **five words or fewer.**
(words like "the, in, a, an, and, to" don't count)

Company Attitude		Write 5 words or fewer
.01	What type of company do you have? What do you offer?	5 words
.02	What differentiates your business from your competitors?	5 words
.03	What type of customer satisfaction do you strive to deliver?	5 words
.04	How do you express your company's vision to your customers	5 words

These answers can be used in your marketing materials.

01. **Byline:** A brief description of what you provide that can be placed next to your company name or logo.

    Guided Business Plan: An entrepreneur-education firm

02. **Slogan:** This is a tag line that gives a reason why someone should be interested in what you offer.

    "Write a business plan in under 20 hours!"

03. **Mantra:** This phrase may describe your vision for your company.

    To motivate entrepreneurs to invest in pre-planning.

04. **Motto:** A phrase to describe how you conduct business.

    Easy, Simple. Guided.

Action Item 12.01 Delegate Your Business

How long will this take?
60 minutes

Chapter Overview
If you are a sole-proprietor, it may be too early for you to start thinking about having employees. But maybe you're a small business owner and you are already used to making payroll. Either way, it's important to plan out your personnel needs and the associated costs.

Who Will Help You?

In this chapter you will...

- List job positions
- Compile resumes/bios
- Form an advisory board

Action Item Guidance

Complete the table on the next page to help you plan your staffing needs. The content from Action Item 12.01 is not included in your plan, however, it will help you think about what you should budget for your staff.

When you are done, continue to the next page to create a list of job responsibilities that you will need to launch your business. Include abbreviations and job status (eg. full-time (FT), part-time (PT), Contract (C), Employee (E)). Estimate your salary expenses for each role. If desired, you can include the job responsibilities in your plan.

Organize Your Staffing Needs!

Human Resources   Write 2 to 5 word answers

.01   Which positions are
      essential to run your
      business?

.02   Do you need to hire
      temporary personnel?

.03   Will you offer benefits
      such as health care?

.04   What non-monetary
      benefits will you offer?

.05   How will you process
      timesheets and pay
      your staff? Through a
      third-party payroll
      vendor?

The questions above are used for planning purposes and do not
necessarily need to be included in a paragraph format.

Delegate Your Business

List the job functions needed to run your business in the near future. Estimate how much you will compensate each position during your start-up phase (years 0 to 1), growth (years 2 to 4) and expansion (4 plus years). Specify if the rate is per hour, per week, per month or per year. These roles will become your **Staffing Needs**.

Job Function/ Status (FT/PT)	Responsibilities	Annual Salary		
		Yrs 0-1	Yrs 2-4	Yrs 4+
		$	$	$
		$	$	$
		$	$	$
		$	$	$
		$	$	$
		$	$	$
		$	$	$

Job Function/ Status (FT/PT)	Responsibilities	Annual Salary		
		Yrs 0-1	Yrs 2-4	Yrs 4+
		$	$	$
		$	$	$
		$	$	$
		$	$	$
		$	$	$
		$	$	$
	Total Salary Compensation:	$	$	$

Structure Your Organization

How is your company structured? Who reports to who? Use the diagram below to show your company's hierarchy. You may write the departments or business units that are needed now or in the near future. You may want to create an organization chart to show how the job functions are organized. Even though you may be the only person performing all of the jobs, this is a good exercise to visualize the team that you will be leading.

List Your Departments
Draw connecting lines to show how departments relate to each other.

Organize Your Job Functions
Write the positions and draw connecting lines to show hierarchy.

Action Item 12.02
Management
Experience

How long will this take?
45 minutes

You probably already have a biographical paragraph for each of your key management. If not, you can create a short biography using the tables below. Write the name and job title for each team member. Revise the sentences to form your brief biographies.

CEO/President

Management Biography	Write 2 to 5 word answers
.01 What is this executive's job title and function within your company?	
.02 What are three major accomplishments during their most recent job position?	
.03 What role did they have at their last three job assignments?	
.04 Where did they go to school and what degree did they obtain?	

.05 What experience,
either paid or
volunteer, do they
have that is relevant
for their role at your
company?

Tell Me More... Why is your CEO/president qualified to lead your company? This section will describe your **Management Team**.

Executive #2

Management Biography	Write 2 to 5 word answers
.06 What is this executive's job title and function within your company?	
.07 What are three major accomplishments during their most recent job position?	
.08 What role did they have at their last three job assignments?	
.09 Where did they go to school and what degree did they obtain?	
.010 What experience, either paid or volunteer, do they have that is relevant for their role at your company?	

Management Biography   Write 2 to 5 word answers

Tell Me More... Why is this person qualified to lead your company?
This section will describe your **Management Team.**

Executive #3

Management Biography	Write 2 to 5 word answers
.011 What is this executive's job title and function within your company?	
.012 What are three major accomplishments during their most recent job position?	
.013 What role did they have at their last three job assignments?	
.014 Where did they go to school and what degree did they obtain?	
.015 What experience, either paid or volunteer, do they have that is relevant for their role at your company?	

Management Biography

Tell Me More... Why is this person qualified to lead your company?
This section will describe your **Management Team**.

Action Item 12.03
Sage Advice

How long will this take?
20 minutes

It's a good idea to create an advisory board. Read through the questions below and jot down notes. Afterwards, create a list of people that you would like to ask to be part of your board. Indicate if they have already confirmed their participation or if you need to invite them. Request their resume or CV and include it in your business plan's appendix.

Advisory Board	Write 2 to 5 word answers
.01 Which of your mentors, if any, would you like to ask to be on your Board?	
.02 Which industries do you want to have represented on your Board?	
.03 What do you want to offer your Board for their participation?	
.04 What experience, paid or volunteer, do they have that is relevant for their role at your company?	

Potential Advisory Board Members

Name	Current or Most Recent Job Position	Company

Action Item 13.01
First Impression

How long will this take?
120-240 minutes

Chapter Overview
Achievement is a great high. Putting your ideas on paper makes it seem more real, doesn't it? Typing it up makes it feel even more official. You have just written the foundation for your business plan...the express way.

Are You Ready To Present?

In this chapter you will...

- Transfer your content
- Edit and format your plan
- Proofread your lender-ready plan

Action Item Guidance

Create a lasting impression by formatting your plan. Add the finishing touches such as a table of contents, graphics, appendix, and style formatting. Consider including organization charts, product photos, tables and other ways to visually convey your points.

Download the **GBP Style Sheet** from guidedbusinessplan.com. Open the file and save it on your computer. It includes instructions to help format your plan. You will type your answers from this book under the corresponding section headers and then complete your business plan.

Transfer Notes to an Electronic Document!

This document will become your first draft and it will change as you research your business. Remember to save as you go along and have someone else proofread it when you are done. Consider the following questions as you design your layout.

Capturing the Look	Write 2 to 5 word answers
.01 What are your company's colors?	
.02 Does your presentation style reflect your industry? Corporate? Young entrepreneur? Cutting-edge? Does your audience prefer certain font styles and sizes?	
.03 What title do you want to include on every page, if any?	

Notes

Formatting Instructions

Action Item/Section	Instructions
	Follow the guidance listed below to transfer your notes to the **GBP Style Sheet**. The GBP Style Sheet is a blank outline of your business plan and is not in the same order as the chapters in this book. You may follow the instructions below or type your notes directly under the corresponding headers within each section of the GBP Style Sheet.
01.01 EXECUTIVE SUMMARY Business Concept, Business Model, Market Need, Competitive Position, Management, Market, Operations, Funding Needs, and Exit Strategy	Turn to Action Item #1.01. Type your answers in the corresponding headers under the **Executive Summary** section. Refer to Action Item #8.02 for your Exit Strategy.
02.01 OPERATIONS Operational Summary	Turn to Action Item #2.02 and type your answers in the corresponding headers under the **Operations** section. Since this is a mini-business plan, you may want to include your process flow cycles to visually explain your operations. In a more detailed plan you would include information about your production facilities and offices, distribution channels, inventory management, research and development, technology needs, etc.

Action Item/Section	Instructions
03.01 **INDUSTRY ANALYSIS** Industry Overview, Factors Driving Demand, Industry Trends, Maturity of Industry, Size and Growth, Buying Patterns, Global Economic Factors, Regulatory Issues and Barriers to Entry	Turn to Action Item #3.01 and type your answers in the corresponding headers under the **Industry Analysis** section. Make sure that you have done your research and have added supporting data.
09.02 **SWOT ANALYSIS** SWOT Analysis	Your **SWOT** consists of the bullets you listed in Action Item #9.02. You can type your bullets under the following headings: Strengths, Weaknesses, Opportunities and Threats.
04.01 **TARGET MARKET** Target Market	Turn to Action Item #4.01 and type your answer in the corresponding header under **Target Market**. Use the table under **Target Market Demographics** to visually profile your target consumer. If desired, insert a photograph of someone who exemplifies your market.
05.01/07.01 **MARKETING** Objective, Sales Strategy, Product Strategy, Pricing Strategy, Distribution Strategy, Promotional Strategy	Turn to Action Item #7.01 and type your answers in the corresponding headers under the **Marketing** section. Your promotional strategy consists of the tactics you listed in Action Item #5.01. You can type your tactics under the following heading: Advertising, Online, Relational and Other.

Action Item/Section	Instructions
06.01 / 06.02/ 08.01 **FINANCIAL** Projected Sales Growth, Pro Forma Cash Flow, Balance Sheet, Income Statement, Capital Assets, Break-Even Analysis and Scenarios	Type your answer to Action Item #8.02 Funding Needs in the corresponding header under the **Financials** section. After you derive the price and cost for your products or services, enter them into the **GBP Financials** spreadsheet. Also enter your sales projections and estimated expenses in order to create several financial statements. You should include several charts within your financial section to graphically convey your message. You may copy and paste the sales projections, income statement, cash flow and capital assets charts into your plan from the GBP Financials. Refer to Checklist I: Financial Assumptions to transfer your assumptions to your plan. Having trouble with Excel? Click Office Leverage : : Office Tips on the BizExpress Toolbar.
09.01 COMPETITION Competitive Position, Direct Competitors, Indirect Competitors	Turn to Action Item #9.01 and type your answers in the corresponding headers under the **Competition** section.
10.01 **SUMMARY** Summary, Expansion Opportunities, Keys to Success, Funding Sought and Contact Information	Turn to Action Item #10.01 and type your answers in the corresponding headers under the **Summary** section.

Action Item/Section	Instructions
11.01 **COMPANY BACKGROUND** Company Description, Legal Name(s), Company History, Company Ownership & Legal Structure , Names of Top Management, Location and Geographical Information, Trademarks, Copyright, Domain Name and Other Information, and Products/Services	Turn to Action Item #11.01 and type your answers in the corresponding headers under the **Company Background** section.
12.01 MANAGEMENT Management Team, Advisory Board (if applicable)	Turn to Action Item #12.01 and type your answers in the corresponding headers under the **Management** section.
13.01 **EDITING AND LAYOUT**	Edit and format your content to create a final business plan.
APPENDIX	You may want to include copies of resumes, legal documents, financial statements, and detailed products and services in your appendix. Refer to Checklist K: Application Requirements.

Definitions
Due Diligence &
Checklists

- Are you unsure of a term listed in this book? Refer to the Definitions : : Business Terms section for clarification.

- Want to save time doing online research? The Due Diligence section lists valuable website links to help you easily navigate the web.

- Do you get distracted with new ideas? Write your idea, inspiration or thought on a checklist at the back of this book. Set aside time to return and complete the action item listed on the checklist.

Definitions : : Business Terms

There are numerous books that you can buy or borrow to learn more about business plan writing, starting a business, and other related topics. We have defined a few terms that are listed in this book. It highly recommended that you continue your self-study by reading contemporary perspectives on the art of starting and growing a business.

Audience Insight
What do you know about your customers that may motivate them to spend more? Do service, ingredients, materials or convenience matter? If you know what is important to them, you can differentiate your marketing materials and service delivery.

Business Concept
How would you describe what your company does in one sentence? Your answer would typically be your business concept and would not include details about your specific products or services.

Business Model
The business model describes your revenue streams. You may list the products or product lines that you're going to sell. In simpler terms, it explains how you're going to get paid.

Certification
There are many types of industry-specific certifications. Your business may also qualify as a Minority-, Women-, Disabled or Veteran-owned company which makes you eligible to participate in some Supplier Diversity programs. Check with your local agency to learn the requirements.

Channel Buyers
If you sell your product through a middle person such as a distributor or retailer, you are dealing with channel buyers. These are people you have to sell to before reaching your end consumer.

Commission
This is a percentage of the sale paid to a sales representative who brokered the deal or to someone who referred that business to you. Commission is calculated on the sales price, either gross or net. Even

though it's not directly factored into your price, you should keep it in mind when determining your product's pricing.

Consumer Market
Your consumer market is another way to describe your customer base. Who are you selling to?

Debt Funding
This is the amount of money you will borrow from a lender.

Demographics
These are characteristics to describe a group based on factors such as economics, lifestyle, education, geography, etc.

Development Phase
Companies just starting out are considered *start-up*. Those that have been in business for a couple of years and have generated significant revenue are considered *seed* companies. Businesses that start a different product line, acquire a subsidiary or have considerable revenue are in an *expansion* phase.

Direct Competition
Think of your direct competition as an entity that sells the same type of product that you sell. Someone who markets $5 beaded necklaces may directly compete with another designer that sells $15 beaded necklaces. Most likely that person is not a direct competitor with a diamond jeweler.

Distribution Channels
This describes how you will get your product from the manufacturer to the end consumer. A food manufacturer may sell their product to a distributor who sells it to a retailer who sells it to an individual customer.

Distributor
A distributor is part of the sales channel. Distributors make it easier for a small company to get their product to many retail outlets. For example, it would be hard for a book publisher to send their book to every book store in their target market. Instead, they can send a large number directly to a distributor who will send the publisher's book and books from other publishers to many stores.

Due Diligence
This term is "corporate speak" for doing your homework to find out more about a subject or project.

Elevator Pitch
Can you summarize your business concept and what you are looking for in less than 30 seconds? This is typically the amount of time you would have in an elevator to pitch an investor, customer or potential stakeholder.

Equity Funding
This is the amount that you may receive from an investor. An "equity stake" or share refers to the percentage of your company that the other party will own if they invest in it.

Exit Strategy
Most investors and lenders want to know what your long-term plans are for your company. Options include selling it, making it a public company or passing it on to an heir.

Freight
Freight is the cost to ship raw goods and finished products to you or to a distributor or a retailer. This is different from shipping directly to a consumer. For example, your printer may ship books to you that you will send to your customers. The cost to send the books to you is considered freight.

Indirect Competition
Think of your indirect competition as an entity that sells similar product(s). A jewelry designer indirectly competes with anyone who sells jewelry.

Labor Costs
Labor is the amount that you have to pay someone (including yourself) to make a product or to deliver the service. To figure out your labor costs, determine how much time it takes to make one unit. If you charge by the hour, then a unit is an hour. If you produce a product, determine how many units you can make per hour. If you can make 5 widgets in an hour, then it takes 12 minutes to make each widget. To calculate the labor cost, multiply the hourly labor rate by the actual time (fraction of an hour) it takes to make each widget. For example, if you have to pay someone $10 per hour to make 5 widgets per hour, then the labor cost per widget is $2. Cost divided by products per hour ($10/5 units per hour).

Legal Structures
There are several types of legal structures that entrepreneurs choose based on cost, risk tolerance, corporate governance and tax implications. A *Sole-proprietor* is the sole owner. Their business income is taxed as their personal income. A *Partnership* is the same as a sole-proprietor except

there are two or more people involved. A *Limited Liability Corporation* is the most popular structure because the business is taxed separately from personal income. The owner's liability is limited to their business assets. A *Corporation* is the most costly and has stringent filing requirements. Management and the board of directors are not personally liable for the business. Consult with a tax professional for advice on which business structure is best for your company.

Market Segmentation
The process of dividing your target market into groups based on similar attributes, likes or dislikes. A grocery store may divide their produce customers into organic buyers and budget-conscious buyers.

Material Costs
This is the price of the raw materials and finished goods that are going into your product. For example, the material costs for baked goods are the costs of the ingredients to make them.

Maturity of Industry
This describes how long an industry has been around. Online TV is a new industry while the banking industry is an extremely mature industry.

NAICS Codes
The North American Industry Classification System (NAICS) was developed to effectively categorize industries. The BizExpress Toolbar lists a website to lookup an industry's code. Your industry code is typically only referenced on legal and/or financial documents.

Non-Monetary Benefits
Employers may compensate employees with incentives other than money such as parking, stock options, complimentary meals, health club memberships, flexible work schedules, etc.

Packaging Costs
You may choose to place your product in a special bag that has your company name or to deliver your product in a special container like a basket. Typically, whatever you pay for your product's container would go under this category. These costs are separate from your shipping and handling costs.

Product Unit and Bundle Pricing

A unit is typically a single item. However, a unit could be a combination product that is sold together like a pair of gloves or earrings. Two singular items sold ("bundled") together like a necklace set with earrings and a necklace should be priced as separate units.

Products versus Services

Products are the physical items that you may sell and services are the action or knowledge that you provide in exchange for compensation. The term "Products" may be used throughout this book to refer to either products or services.

Profit Margin

The profit margin is a standard financial calculation that shows how much money a company keeps for each dollar that they earn in sales. A 35% profit margin would indicate that a company makes 35 cents for each dollar in revenue.

Return on Investment (ROI)

The ROI is a standard term to determine the benefit(s) of an investment. An investor may want to ensure that they receive $1.20 for every $1.00 that they invest since they are willing to take a risk. A marketer may want to receive 10 new customers for every 1,000 postcards that they send out. ROIs will vary based on the situation and the decision makers.

Revenue Streams

This is a way to categorize the money that a company generates from selling various products or services. A coffee house may make money selling beverages, but they could also rent out their space for local events. Drink sales and office rental are two types of revenue streams.

Trademarks, Patents and Copyright

The above terms are ways to protect your intellectual property—any work that you have created. A logo, slogan or something else that identifies your company can be trademarked. You can protect it so others cannot make money from selling items with your trademark. Trademarks take a long time to process through the United States Patent and Trademark Office (USPTO). Patent registration takes even longer than trademarks. You can protect a unique procedure or invention that you have created by applying for a patent to prove your ownership. A copyright is used to protect material that you have created like a book, song lyrics or artwork. Copyrights are generated once the work is created, but it is recommended to legally register any work via the US Copyright Office.

Unique Selling Proposition (USP)

Your USP is a phrase that differentiates your product from what exists in the marketplace. It is a clear way to explain why your product will benefit the customer.

Vet

A term used to describe performing a thorough background review of a person, company or project.

Volume Discount

Discounts for purchasing items in bulk.

Wholesaler

A wholesaler is part of the sales channel. They will buy your product at a discounted rate and then sell it at a price above what they paid for it. Most retailers are wholesalers because they have a location where people can buy the product and therefore are rewarded with volume discounts.

BOOK SAMPLE

GUIDED BUSINESS PLAN
"A Goal Without a Plan Is Just a Wish."

Due Diligence : : Online Action Items

The Guided Business Plan™ lists several website recommendations below. Links change and some websites become obsolete so we decided not to directly list the site address in this book. Instead we have posted them on an easy-to-access format: an online toolbar. We encourage you to download the free toolbar from guidedbusinessplan.com. Once it is part of your browser, you can click on the Category Name and then the Link Name to access a great resource.

Company Start-up

Find available domain names.
BP : : Biz Start-up | Domain Availability

Verify that your company name is not being used by someone else.
BP : : Biz Start-up | Name Lookup

Verify that your name does not infringe on an existing trademark. Learn more about trademarks, patents and copyrights.
BP : : Biz Start-up | Trademarks and Patents
BP : : Biz Start-up | Free Patent Search
BP : : Biz Start-up | Copyright Office

Business registration.
BP : : Biz Start-up | Apply for EIN
BP : : Biz Start-up | Register a Business
BP : : Biz Start-up | Register FBN
BP : : Biz Start-up | Publish FBN

Discover what licenses and permits are required for your business.
BP : : Biz Start-up | Licenses & Permits
BP : : Biz Start-up | Biz Forms by State

Compare legal business structures.
BP : : Biz Start-up | Setup LLC or Corp

Operations	Hold online meetings for free or low cost.
	BP : : Business Tools | Free Conferencing 1
	BP : : Business Tools | Free Conferencing 2
	BP : : Startup Vendors | Go To Meeting
	Create assessment and evaluation surveys.
	BP : : Business Tools | Online Survey 1
	BP : : Business Tools | Online Survey 2
	Setup a toll-free number or a public one.
	BP : : Start-up Vendors | Toll-free Number Search
	BP : : Start-up Vendors | 1-800 Phone Number
	BP : : Start-up Vendors | Public Phone Number
	Open up a public mailbox.
	BP : : Start-up Vendors | Earth Class
	Find short-term office rentals.
	BP : : Start-up Vendors | Daily Office Rental
	Create a website.
	BP : : Start-up Vendors | Website in a Box
Industry Overview	Search for information about your industry or business type.
	BP : : Research Tools | Reference for Business
	BP : : Research Tools | Industry Search Starter
	BP : : Research Tools | Periodical Search
	BP : : Research Tools | Google Finance
	BP : : Research Tools | Mantra: Company Profiles
	BP : : Research Tools | Hoovers
	BP : : Research Tools | Yahoo Finance
	BP : : Research Tools | SIC Codes
	BP : : Research Tools | Answers
	BP : : Research Tools | Wikipedia
Target Market / Size & Growth	Research statistics about your market.
	BP : : Research Tools | City Data
	BP : : Research Tools | Vital Stats
	BP : : Research Tools | Census Data

BP : : Research Tools | Corp Info
BP : : Research Tools | Population Maps
BP : : Research Tools | Melissa Data
BP : : Research Tools | Demographics by Zip Code
BP : : Research Tools | Ethnic American Markets

Competition

Compare your web traffic.
BP : : Research Tools | Quantcast
BP : : Research Tools | Alexa

Lookup company profiles.
BP : : Research Tools | Reference for Business *
BP : : Research Tools | Inc. Private Companies
BP : : Research Tools | Yelp
BP : : Research Tools | Annual Reports

*Click "Company Histories" on this web page

Marketing Ideas

An online portfolio to showcase your products.
BP : : Image Builder | Online Portfolio
BP : : Business Tools | Customer Community

Broadcast your message online.
BP : : Image Builder | Broadcast Live

Create gift cards with your logo.
BP : : Image Builder | Branded Gift Cards 1

Get ideas for online marketing campaigns.
BP : : Image Builder | Video Email
BP : : Image Builder | Email Marketing

Promote your business via online classifieds.
BP : : Image Builder | Google Classifieds
BP : : Image Builder | Kijiji Classifieds

Advertise on TV.
BP : : Image Builder | Spot Runner
BP : : Image Builder | Retail Advertising

Layout	Learn how to apply styles to your Word document. BP : : Office Leverage | Styles Learn how to format headers and footers within your Word document. BP : : Office Leverage | Headers & Footers Learn how to format a Table of Contents. BP : : Office Leverage | Table of Contents Microsoft Office® step by step instructions. BP : : Office Leverage | Office Tips
Monetize Content	Supplement your business with affiliate marketing or by monetizing your content (receive payments for creative content downloads). BP : : Monetize Content | Books BP : : Monetize Content | Articles BP : : Monetize Content | Videos BP : : Monetize Content | Magazines BP : : Monetize Content | Photos
Supply Sources	Purchase inventory for resale. BP : : Supply Sources | Doba (Inventory on Demand) BP : : Supply Sources | Liquidation BP : : Supply Sources | Global Suppliers BP : : Supply Sources | Wholesale Links

Checklist Summary

Overview : : Organize your to-do list with these checklists.
You may download the GBP Checklists from guidedbusinessplan.com.

Checklist A: Budget : : Keep track of your expenses as you think of them. Use this checklist to complete your Financials spreadsheet.

Checklist B: Operations : : Write down tools that you will need to operate your business and then set aside time later to develop them.

Checklist C: Marketing Collateral : : List the marketing items that you need to promote your business.

Checklist D & E & F: Milestones : : Write down a summary of the goals you will accomplish each month for start-up, marketing and production phases.

Checklist G: Research : : Track the research you need to look up or confirm in order to support your statements.

Checklist H: General : : Got an idea? Write it down and address it later. Don't get distracted from the task you are currently working on.

Checklist I: Financial Assumptions : : List the assumptions you are making as you develop your financial statements.

Checklist J: Vendors & Suppliers : : Maintain a list of vendors that you would like to work with.

Checklist K: Application Requirements : : Assemble all of the materials you may need to present to a lender or an investor.

Checklist A
Budget

Guidance
As you complete this workbook, you may think of an expense that you will incur. List it here and then include it in your budget once you're ready to work on that section.

Budget Checklist

Item	Vendor	Est. Price	Phase Needed

Budget Checklist

Item	Vendor	Est. Price	Phase Needed

Checklist B
Operations

Guidance

Keep a list of the tools that you will need to run your business. For example, you may need to have a database to track clients or a software package for your accounting system. We have included examples below.

Operations Checklist

Item	Group	Notes
Client tracking database	Operations/ Accounting	
Accounting software	Operations/ Accounting	
Website	Operations	
Toll-free number	Operations	

Operations Checklist

Item	Group	Notes

Checklist C
Marketing Collateral

Guidance

As you develop your business plan, you may think of the materials that you're going to use to market your company such as brochures, business cards, text for emails, etc. Write down the promotional items you will need to create. We have included a few examples.

Marketing Collateral Checklist

Item	Type	Due Date	Complete?	Notes
E-newsletter to introduce company	Electronic newsletter			
E-newsletter to follow-up interest	Electronic newsletter			
Postcards	Printed material			
Business cards	Printed material			

Marketing Collateral Checklist

Item	Type	Due Date	Complete?	Notes

Checklist D
Milestones: Start-up

Guidance
Use this checklist to summarize what you hope to accomplish each month during the first year and then annually for the second year.

Start-up Milestones Checklist

Month	Activity or Goals
Ongoing	
January	
February	
March	

Start-up Milestones Checklist

Month	Activity or Goals
April	
May	
June	
July	
August	

Start-up Milestones Checklist

Month	Activity or Goals
September	
October	
November	
December	
Year 2	

Checklist E
Milestones: Marketing

Guidance
Use this checklist to summarize the marketing activities you plan to accomplish each month.

Marketing Milestones Checklist

Month	Activity or Goals
Ongoing	
January	
February	
March	

Marketing Milestones Checklist

Month	Activity or Goals
April	
May	
June	
July	
August	

Marketing Milestones Checklist

Month	Activity or Goals
September	
October	
November	
December	

Checklist F
Milestones: Production

Guidance

Use this checklist to summarize the activities that you need to accomplish each month in order to produce your product or service.

Production Milestones Checklist

Month	Activity or Goals
Ongoing	
January	
February	
March	

Production Milestones Checklist

Month	Activity or Goals
April	
May	
June	
July	
August	

Production Milestones Checklist

Month	Activity or Goals
September	
October	
November	
December	

Checklist G
Research

Guidance
Use this list to track topics that you need to research to support statements in your business plan.

Research Checklist

Action Item Number or Topic or Page #	Research Item

Research Checklist

Action Item Number or Topic or Page #	Research Item

Checklist H
General

Guidance
When inspiration hits, write it down. Keep a checklist to help you organize your work.

General Checklist

Idea	Category	Date Due

General Checklist

Idea	Category	Date Due

Checklist I
Financial Assumptions

Guidance
As you develop your financial statements, it's important to keep a list of the assumptions you are basing your calculations on. For example, you may assume that demand for your product will increase by 5% each year therefore your sales may increase by 1% each year. Include these assumptions within your Financials.

Financial Assumptions Checklist

Category	Assumptions
Sales	
Cash Flow	
Personnel	

Financial Assumptions Checklist

Category	Assumptions
Break-Even Analysis	
Income Statement	
Balance Sheet	
Other	

Checklist J
Vendors & Suppliers

Guidance
Place a check mark next to the vendor function that you may need and write down a company or contact name. As you research the internet or attend networking events, you may come across a vendor that you would like to use now or in the near future. You can track those vendors on the list below.

Vendors & Suppliers Checklist

☑	Function	Group	Company/ Contact Name	Notes
☐	Accountant	Financial		
☐	Bank	Operations		
☐	Business Development/ Business Incubator Center	Start-up		
☐	Call Center	Operations		
☐	Emarketing/Online Newsletters	Operations		
☐	Internet Marketing	Marketing		
☐	Legal	Legal		

Vendors & Suppliers Checklist

☑	Function	Group	Company/ Contact Name	Notes
☐	Mailing Address	Operations		
☐	Merchant Account	Operations		
☐	Office Space	Operations		
☐	Printing	Operations		
☐	Publicist	Marketing		
☐	Researchers	Market Research		
☐	Sales Lead Lists	Marketing		
☐	Toll-Free Number	Operations		
☐	Web Developer	Operations		
☐	Web Host	Operations		
☐				
☐				

Vendors & Suppliers Checklist

☑	Function	Group	Company/ Contact Name	Notes
☐				
☐				
☐				
☐				
☐				
☐				
☐				
☐				
☐				
☐				
☐				
☐				

Checklist K
Application Requirements

Guidance

Make a list of all items that are needed to process your loan application or documents that may be required by an investor. You may need tax returns for the last three years so indicate the length of time required under "Time Duration". Place a checklist next to the ones that are required.

Application Requirements Checklist

Item	Req?	Time Duration	☑?	Notes
Business financial statements (profit and loss, cash flow, break-even)	☐			
Business tax returns	☐			
Notarized statements	☐			
List of current debt	☐			
Articles of Incorporation	☐			
Partnership Agreement	☐			

Application Requirements Checklist

Item	Req?	Time Duration	☑?	Notes
Fictitious Business Name statement	❑			
Proof of liability insurance	❑			
Lease documents	❑			
Collateral documents	❑			
Resumes of key management	❑			
Personal financial statements/tax returns	❑			
Pending customer orders	❑			
Patents, trademarks, copyright notices	❑			
	❑			

Style Sheet Outline

One of the goals of the Guided Business Plan™ is to translate business terms into everyday language for those who have little experience building a business. In the first chapter you answered the what, why, who, where and how of your business plan. You were also writing the business concept, market need, competitive position, market summary and funding needs. The following is the structure of your final business plan if you use the **GBP Style Sheet** that accompanies this book. You may download the file for free from www.guidedbusinessplan.com.

EXECUTIVE SUMMARY

Business Concept

Business Model

Market Need

Competitive Position

Management

Market

Operations

Funding Needs

Exit Strategy

COMPANY BACKGROUND

Company Overview

Mission Statement

Legal Names

Company Ownership & Legal Structure

Names of Top Management

Location and Geographical Information

Trademarks, Copyright, Domain Name and Other Information

Products/Services

INDUSTRY OVERVIEW

Industry Overview

Market Drivers

Industry Trends

Maturity of Industry

Size and Growth

Buying Patterns

Global Economic Factors

Regulatory Issues

Barriers to Entry

SWOT ANALYSIS

Strengths

Weaknesses

Opportunities

Threats

TARGET MARKET

Target Market Demographics

COMPETITION

Competitive Position

Direct Competitors

Indirect Competitors

MARKETING

Objective

Sales Strategy

Product Strategy

Pricing Strategy

Distribution Strategy

Promotional Strategy

Advertising

Online

Relational

Other

OPERATIONS

Operation Summary

Operation Process

MANAGEMENT SUMMARY

Staffing Needs

Management Team

Advisory Board

FINANCIALS

Sales Projections

Income Statement

Balance Sheet

Cash Flow

Capital Assets

Funding Needs

SUMMARY

Summary

Expansion Opportunities

Keys to Success

Funds Sought

Contact Information

APPENDIX

Notes

Write down any ideas or inspiration that you need to add to an action list later.

Notes

Write down any ideas or inspiration that you need to add to an action list later.

Notes

Write down any ideas or inspiration that you need to add to an action list later.

Notes

Write down any ideas or inspiration that you need to add to an action list later.

About Us

Guided Business Plan: an entrepreneur-education firm

Even the big 3 automakers need a business plan.

During the 2008 bailout hearings, Congress requested a business plan from GM, Ford and Chrysler before approving funding. As their loan officer, the government wanted to know how the funds would help grow the business. In a recessionary economy, there are thousands of similar loan officers who are requesting the same documents from first-time and seasoned entrepreneurs.

Guided Business Plan is a company devoted to equipping entrepreneurs with free to low-cost resources and guidance to create their business plan.

About the Author

Melanie Rae is a Massachusetts native who has lived in Los Angeles, California for over a decade. She credits the career development organization INROADS® with providing her first exposure to flourishing in a business environment. Melanie hopes to have a similar impact by inspiring at least 50,000 people to release the entrepreneur within. She created the Guided Business Plan community website for new entrepreneurs to register and promote their company. She believes that with educated determination anyone can turn their dreams into action and then into a success story.

GUIDED
BUSINESS PLAN